MW00713916

Developing LeanSigma® Leaders
Pocket Guide

Principles, Tools,
Checklists and Agendas for Running Successful
Flow Production, Business Process,
Sigma Kaizen and Design for LeanSigma events

Developing LeanSigma® Leaders
Pocket Guide

A companion to *Developing LeanSigma Leaders:
A Workbook for Kaizen Breakthrough Leadership*

By TBM Consulting Group, Inc.

Contributors: Janet Barbato, J.D. Cunningham, Carl
Deeley, Dan Gallagher, Matt Goesling, Dave Hensley,
Tom Morin, Bonnie Smith, Dan Sullivan, Noel
Temple, Joe Tipton, Bob Wenning

Editor/writer: Emily Adams
Concept/Course Design: Bob Dean
Book Design: Amy Robbins, IONA design

Managing Times Press
4400 Ben Franklin Boulevard
Durham, NC 27704

© **2004 TBM Consulting Group, Inc**
All rights reserved. No part of this book may be reproduced by
any means electronic or mechanical without written
permission from the publisher.

TBM Consulting Group, Inc. is sole licensee of LeanSigma®, a
registered service mark of Maytag Corporation.

Foreword

A kaizen team is the front line of a company's
LeanSigma transformation. As the team leader,
you need to stay at least two hours ahead of your
team, preparing for every possibility. In the heat
of a kaizen week, it's easy to forget certain tools
and deadlines. This book is designed to help keep
you on track, with the schedules, principles and
tools of a kaizen week. Use it in conjunction with
the *Developing LeanSigma Leaders* workbook to
help guide you through the challenges and
rewards of a kaizen week.

Leading a kaizen breakthrough team can change
the shape of your career and the fortunes of your
business. Be prepared for hard work and plan
ahead. Good luck.

Flow Production & Business Process

• Princples & Tools •

Checklists & Agendas
Flow Production, Business Process

Value-Added

A value-added activity transforms materials and information into products or services that the customer wants and will pay for.

Non Value-Added

Activities that consume resources without contributing to the product or service.

Takt Time

A frequently misused term, takt time is simply the rate of customer demand. If consumers require 220 products in a day, takt time for the plant is calculated based on the available time worked during the day. If the plant works one shift and a shift has 440 minutes of production time (eight hours, minus 30 minutes for breaks and 10 minutes for end-of-shift cleanup), then the takt time is two minutes.

Or, if an order entry department receives 275 orders per day and the time available to process the orders is 440 minutes (eight hours, minus 30 minutes for breaks and 10 minutes for pre-shift meetings), takt time is 440 minutes, times 60 seconds, divided by 275 orders. So takt time equals 96 seconds per order.

The 7 Wastes: Flow Production

1. Defects or corrections are the most easily recognized form of waste. Re-work is always categorized as waste, which the lean organization seeks to eliminate.

2. Overproduction is making too much of anything. This usually occurs because some machines are faster than others, or are run faster to optimize an investment.

3. Inventory, whether it is raw material, work in process (WIP) or finished goods, is almost always waste. Some WIP inventory is required between process steps to keep the flow of production moving. This should be carefully controlled, however, and limited to the essential needs of the operation.

4. Excess motion is any movement outside of the immediate needs of the work. Walking around looking for tools or new work materials, or entering data twice is waste.

5. Over processing occurs when a single piece of material is put through multiple processes to achieve a single goal.

6. Transporting materials is usually a good indi cation that a batch and queue mentality is still in place because transportation rarely involves a single piece at a time.

7. Waiting is always time lost, whether you are waiting for people, material, processes or machines.

The 7 Wastes: Business Process

1. Errors and resulting re-work are the most easily recognized form of waste. Re-work is always categorized as waste.

2. Overproduction is processing too much of anything. This usually occurs because some machines or people are faster than others.

3. Backlog & In-process items – whether a backlog of transactions, a pile of paperwork or things partially completed – are a form of waste. This category is often the root cause of mistakes and always results in longer lead times and dissatisfied customers.

4. Excess motion is any movement outside of the immediate needs of the work. Walking around looking for new work materials or entering data twice is waste, as is bending, stretching and searching.

5. Over processing occurs when there is more work done than is required to satisfy the request. This often happens because "it's always been done this way."

6. Transporting paper is usually a good

indication that a batch and queue mentality is still in place because transportation rarely involves a single piece at a time.

7. Waiting is always time lost, whether you are waiting for people, information, processes or machines.

Cycle Time
The amount of time it takes to complete a work cycle, proceeding at a normal pace.

Pull
In a true pull system, the customer is in control of production. The plant is triggered to replenish and suppliers are alerted to deliver more material as the customer pulls from stock. This is the goal of every lean organization.

Flow
When we refer to flow, we always mean one-piece or one-unit flow. Improvements should always move production away from batch processing and toward a flow in which each piece or unit moves through the plant or office without unnecessary waiting or transportation. In this way, we force attention to the process itself, instead of to side issues, such as transporting, waiting, etc.

Kaizen Newspaper

This is used whenever a series of tasks are
assigned to make sure that tasks, responsibilities
and deadlines are clear. Always fill in the kaizen
newspaper in front of the team to ensure that
everyone understands and accepts the tasks and
timelines.

What	Who	When	Expected Results	3/14 Progress
*Comp Machine Axis	*Shaun/ Eddie Carter	*3/8	*MTS to comp axis	*Complete 3/13
OEM issues	Rich Wasman	3/14	OEM to respond back with plan to implement	Working: Not Getting Response from Vendor
*Tacking Fixture	*Sosa	*3/14	*Prototype developed and TDR submitted	*Waiting on Tack welder configuration information
Tabulate WTL cutup data	Hutch	3/14	Ongoing for OEM visit 4/11	Working
Submit mount to MPE for SEM analysis	Rich	3/14	Submitted to MPE and working	Need to get mounts from Eng. E-sect. Expect 3/27
Vision system cover finder repeatability tests, glued-tacked-formed	Sosa/Rich	3/14	Results from 1 part loaded 10X for each situation. Must happen after axis comp.	Waiting on Axis Comp. 3/21

* Indicates may need management priority/support

Time Observation Form

This lists each step in a work cycle, the time it
takes to complete the step and any additional
observations.

Process:								Observer:							Date:	
Step	Operation Element	1	2	3	4	5	6	7	8	9	10	11	12	Task Time	Remarks
1	Stand up from Chair	06	53	38	23	13	54	42	29	17	7'02	51			
2	Walk to Blackboard	18	1'04	48	34	23	8'06	53	40	27	13	8'01			
3	Pick up Chalk	20	06	51	37	25	09	55	43	29	16	04			
4	Write on Board	30	15	2'01	48	34	M	5'05	53	38	27	15			
5	Put down Chalk	33	18	05	51	37	23	09	56	41	31	18			
6	Walk back to Chair	43	27	14	3'01	46	32	19	6'06	52	40	28			
7	Sit down	46	30	16	04	48	35	22	09	54	42	31			
	Time for 1 Cycle														

Observe and time the process through several iterations, then note the lowest repeatable cycle time in the bottom row.

Cycle Time/Takt Time Bar Chart

Takt Time = $\dfrac{\text{Net available operating time}}{\text{Customer requirements}}$ = $\dfrac{240" \text{ per day}}{6 \text{ units per day}}$ = 40" per unit

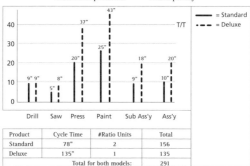

Product	Cycle Time	#Ratio Units	Total
Standard	78"	2	156
Deluxe	135"	1	135
	Total for both models:		291

Total/#of Units=Weighted Average Cycle Time (291 ÷ 3 = 97" per unit)

Weighted Cycle Time ÷ Takt Time = # of Operators (97" per unit ÷ 40" per unit = 2.4 Operators)

Draw a dotted line across the top, showing takt time for the process. Vertical lines, up from the bottom, show each operator's cycle time. Note the cycle time in seconds or minutes for each operator by function (e.g. base assembly, attach fan).

Spaghetti Diagram

Step	Problems												
1.													
2.													
3.													
4.													
5.													
6.													
7.													
8.													
9.													
10.													
11.													
12.													

One of the best ways to reveal a poorly laid out work cycle, the spaghetti diagram will help team members imagine new layouts. Make sure each step in the process is written out at left, with recurrent problems noted.

Common Tools

Standard Operations

This form should be completed for each operator or clerk, documenting all facets of the improved work cycle.

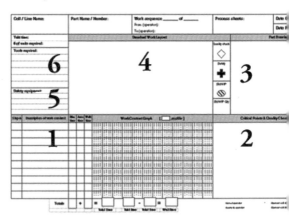

1 Note each step in the work cycle, including cycle times for manual labor, machine labor & walking.

Step #	Description of work content	Man time	Auto time	Walk time
1	Snap legs and plastic cover together	5		1
2	Snap casters in place	8		2
3	Assemble stand & legs	5		1
4	Put telescopic cover on	5		
5	Attach spring to spring knob	5		
6	Attach knob to small bracket	10		
7	Attach small bracket to large bracket	28		2
	Totals	**62**	**+**	**6**

2 Sketch critical quality or safety issues within the work cycle.

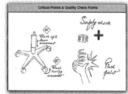

3 Draw each part, in the correct assembly sequence. The key is for symbols used throughout the document.

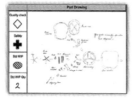

4 Sketch the entire work station, showing the expected movement of materials and operator. Remember, we're looking for flow.

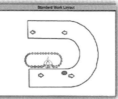

5 List necessary safety equipment.

Safety equipment:
Safety shoes
Safety goggles

6 Note all tools needed for operation.

Tools required:
Screw gun
3/8" Open-ended wrench
Screw driver

Staffing Matrix

Use this tool if the process suffers wide swings in demand from seasonal variation or other reasons. This Excel file is found on the CD attached to the back cover of the *Developing LeanSigma Leaders* workbook, in the Flow Production folder.

Output/shift	Operators Required	Takt Time
250	2	108
Operator 1		15
	Attach hardware to top side of unit	15
	Install pads	10
	Place lock	12
	Place top plate	13
	Apply gold tape	15
	Pop rivet top plate	18
	Move unit to next station	8
Operator 2	Total Cycle Time	106
	Apply 2 corner caps to front	12
	Apply 2 corner caps to back	17
	Install 3 label onto frame of unit	24
	Install corner brace with foam	14
	Install center divider	10
	Screw middle hinge	10
	Place duct on unit	9
	Move cabinet to next station	8
	Total Cycle Time	104

Output/shift	Operators Required	Takt Time
350	3	77
Operator 1	Steps	Cycle Time
	Attach hardware to top side of unit	15
	Attach hardware to top side of unit	15
	Install pads	10
	Place lock	12
	Place top plate	13
	Move unit to next station	8
Operator 2	Total Cycle Time	73
	Pop rivet top plate	18
	Apply gold tape	15
	Apply 2 corner caps to front	12
	Apply 2 corner caps to back	17
	Move unit to next station	8
Operator 3	Total Cycle Time	70
	Install corner brace with foam	14
	Install center divider piece	10
	Screw middle hinge	10
	Place duct on unit	7
	Install 3 labels onto frame of unit	24
	Total Cycle Time	67

Output/shift	Operators Required	Takt Time
450	4	60
Operator 1	Attach hardware to bottom side of unit	15
	Attach hardware to top side of unit	15
	Install pads	10
	Move unit to next station	
	Total Cycle Time	48
Operator 2	Apply gold tape	15
	Apply 2 corner caps to front	12
	Place lock	12
	Place top plate	13
	Total Cycle Time	52
Operator 3	Install corner brace with foam	14
	Pop rivet top plate	18
	Apply 2 corner caps to back	17
	Move unit to next station	8
	Total Cycle Time	57
Operator 4	Install center divider piece	10
	Screw middle hinge	10
	Place duct on unit	9
	Install 3 labels onto frame of unit	24
	Total Cycle Time	53

Break down each operator's jobs into tasks, note the cycle time of each task, then use the embedded formulas to reconfigure staffing for variations in takt time.

5S

A Japanese term that was created by Toyota Production System architects, 5S is a methodology for creating and maintaining a clean, organized workplace. It is also one of the most important

conditioning excercises of LeanSigma. The defi-
nition of each "S" is noted below, with the
Japanese and English terms. It's important to note
that these activities are meant to be carried out
in the order written.

> Seiri (sort): segregrate and discard
> Seiton (set in order): arrange and identify
> Seiso (sweep up): clean and inspect daily
> Seiketsu (standardize): revisit frequently
> Shitsuke (sustain): motivate to sustain

5S Process: Step by step
1. Observe, interview people in area, evaluate.
2. Establish a quarrantine area.
3. Red tag the area.
4. Review summary sheet with area associates.
5. Determine if additional resources are needed.
6. Clean up entire project area.
7. Conduct another observation.
8. Evaluate area with 5S Score Sheet.
9. Conduct root-cause analysis; establish
   countermeasures.
10. Repeat steps 6-8 to improve score.
11. Post evaluation on performance board.
12. Determine 5S auditing cycle.

Red Tags

Machine Name: Okuma LC20 B-344

No.	Malfunction	Action	Who	When	OK
1	Oil leak	Need chute designed to guide and catch way lube oil	Maint.	4/18/91	
2	Metal filter cover over the pump screen bent	Straighten or replace	Team	4/10/91	Complete
3	Two screws missing on way cover housing	Replace	Team	4/18/91	Complete
4	Roller bearing missing on the top track of the sliding door	Replace	Maint.	4/21/91	
5	Oil leak at the base of the Nachi hydraulic pump	Check gasket, replace if needed	Maint.	5/13/91	

Use red tags to mark items for removal and track disposition. Make sure team members fill out tags completely, explaining the need for each item's removal. A few tips for successful 5S:

- Be fair. Tag all areas, not just the obvious ones.
- Don't compromise. When in doubt, move it out.
- One tag per item.
- Tag items deemed necessary, if improvements are suggested.
- Don't red tag people.
- Be reasonable regarding decorative or personal items.

5S Audits

Auditing should be a part of every workplace practice, to reinforce the benefits of 5S, such as standard work and safety. Each employee should

have a daily 5S checklist, but this does not pre-
clude regular audits.

Note: All n/a items automatically receive the high score. Area: _____
Date: _____

Segregate & Discard	Check Score					Remarks
Trash can & recycling bin present	1	2	3	4	5	
Floor is clear of junk	1	2	3	4	5	
Work surface materials (including files) are current	2	4	6	8	10	
Notes on walls are current & relevent to work	1	2	3	4	5	
Materials on bookshelf / cabinet are relevent to work	1	2	3	4	5	
Subtotals (checked scores)						
Total for Segregate & Discard (Available = 30)						

Arrange & Identify	Check Score					Remarks
Bookshelf / cabinet materials labeled	1	2	3	4	5	
Inventory is posted on outside of cabinet (common areas)	1	2	3	4	5	
All files & file drawers are labeled	2	4	6	8	10	
Standard procedures are posted for all equipment	2	4	6	8	10	
Standard work procedures for occupant are posted	2	4	6	8	10	
Subtotals (checked scores)						
Total for Arrange & Identify (Available = 40)						

Clean & Orderly	Check Score					Remarks
Furniture & equipment is clean & orderly	1	2	3	4	5	
Floor, walls, cabinets, shelves, & work surfaces are clean	1	2	3	4	5	
Cabinets, shelves, & work surfaces are orderly	1	2	3	4	5	
Files on work surface & in file drawers are orderly	1	2	3	4	5	
Personal items are orderly & appropriate for office	1	2	3	4	5	
In / out boxes are orderly						
Subtotals (checked scores)						
Total for Clean & Orderly (Available = 30)						

Score Summary:	Total (Available = 100)		
Suggestions:			

For each category listed in the left column, assign
a score for the area being assessed. Use the standard 0-5 scoring as illustrated in the "scoring criteria" at top. Beware grade inflation! It is human
nature to offer praise for hard work with higher
scores than is warranted.

Set-up Reduction
Set-up time is defined as the amount of time it
takes to change over a piece of equipment from
the last good part of production to the first good

piece of the new production lot. Adjustments are not part of set-up time.

Set-up reduction events always follow a basic script, with each element of work leading logically to the next. Teams should run through the work cycle more than once during an event.

Set-up Reduction Observation Time

Begin by documenting each step of an equipment changeover, noted in the left column. The "finish time" column denotes the point in the total set-up cycle in which this step is finished. The total time for this step is also noted, along with tools or gauges used, notes about the process and observations, such as adjustments that are done.

	Start time for this sheet:	16' 15"				
Step #	Element Description	Finish Time	Step Time	Tools / Gauges	Process Info	Observations
51	Bring in cart #1 right side	16' 40"	25"			
52	Bring in cart #2 left side	17' 09"	29"			
53	Get material in place	18' 12"	63"			
54	Run first part	18' 31"	19"			
55	Adjust die height RS	19' 13"	42"	Socket wrench w/ 3/4" socket		Adjustment
56	Drop die	19' 21"	8"			
57	Adjust die height LS	19' 58"	37"	Socket wrench w/ 3/4" socket		Adjustment
58	Finish bolts RS	20' 03"	5"	Socket wrench w/ 5/8" socket		Tightened bolts
59	Cycle die	20' 13"	10"			
60	Remove blank	20' 30"	17"			
61	Load material	20' 38"	8"			
62 63	Cycle Die Remove blank	20' 44"	6"			
64	Inspect part	20' 57"	23"			
		Total	4' 52"			

Overall Equipment Effectiveness

Total Productive Maintenance projects are measured by the Overall Equipment Effectiveness (OEE) score. To figure your OEE score, use the following formulas.

- Available time = Total shift time, minus allowable breaks.
- Downtime = Includes machine set-up time and maintenance or other downtime.
- MCT = Machine cycle time
- Operating time = Available time, minus all downtime.

Example:

Availability = 450 min. – 50 min.)/450 = **0.890**
Perf. = (1 min./part X 350 parts)/400 = **0.875**
Quality = (350 parts – 35 parts)/350 = **0.900**

OEE = 0.890 X 0.875 X 0.900 X 100 = **70%**

Blue Tags (for TPM)

Use blue tags to identify sources of contamination and malfunction, attaching the blue tags to the machine where the problem occurs. Maintenance should receive a copy of each blue tag, while the information from each is entered on the Blue Tag Summary form.

Machine Name: Okuma LC20 B-344

No.	Malfunction	Action	Who	When	OK
1	Oil leak	Need chute designed to guide and catch way lube oil	Maint.	4/18/91	
2	Metal filter cover over the pump screen bent	Straighten or replace	Team	4/10/91	Complete
3	Two screws missing on way cover housing	Replace	Team	4/18/91	Complete
4	Roller bearing missing on the top track of the sliding door	Replace	Maint.	4/21/91	
5	Oil leak at the base of the Nachi hydraulic pump	Check gasket, replace if needed	Maint.	5/13/91	

Management/Team Leader Meetings (All)

The information presented to senior managers during team leader meetings will vary slightly on each day of a kaizen week, as the work progresses. The script, however, is basically unchanging. Here is what you need to say:

Hi, I'm _____ leading the _____ team.

Our objectives are:

The current situation is:

Our plan is:

Barriers encountered include (if relevant):

Any questions?

Flow Production & Business Process

Princples & Tools

• Checklists & Agendas •

Flow Production, Business Process

Flow Production

Agenda: Pre-Event Meeting with KPO

Remember to cover these topics during your pre-event meeting with your KPO event coordinator.

1. Team packets prepared?
2. My objectives:
3. Background on the area
4. Historical data
5. Target area meeting
6. Maintenance worker assigned

Team packets should include:
- Kaizen event objectives
- Area layout
- Process flow diagram
- Number of employees per shift
- Product demand by time of day, day of week, week of month and month of year, as appropriate
- List of area rules and safety procedures

Pre-Event Checklist

✓ Team selected
✓ Team packet prepared
✓ Pre-event meeting held in target area
✓ Historic data collected (scrap, OT, etc.)
✓ Value chain maps sketched
✓ Area visited

✓ Contact made with maintenance
✓ All needed materials available

Pre-event List: TPM

In addition to the regular pre-event checklist, get all data available for the machine including:

- Downtime history
- Quality data
- Daily production
- Manufacturer's technical specifications
- Process specifications

Pre-event List: Set-up Reduction

In addition to the regular pre-event checklist, get all data available for the machine, including:

- Number of changeovers per period (e.g. daily, weekly, etc.)
- Current changeover time
- Number of products or parts across the machine
- Daily demand (P/Q analysis)
- Quality data
- Manufacturer's technical specifications

Kaizen Event Agenda: Flow

Monday	Training
Tuesday	Discovery
Wednesday	Do
Thursday	Do, Re-do, Document
Friday	Debrief

Kaizen Event Agenda: TPM

Monday	Training
Tuesday	Observe, Tag & Clean
Wednesday	Find & Fix
Thursday	Standardize & Teach
Friday	Debrief

Kaizen Event Agenda: Set-up Reduction

Monday	Training
Tuesday	Observe & Separate
Wednesday	Brainstorm & Implement
Thursday	Standardize & Practice
Friday	Debrief

Sample Flow Kaizen Agenda: Tuesday

1. Introduction; review safety rules, current process
2. Tour the target area
3. Review time observation forms; create sub teams
4. Time observation studies
5. Data reports, brainstorming
6. Brainstorming; additional data collection
7. Project selection

Sample Flow Kaizen Agenda: Wednesday

1. Break down the line
2. Move equipment, create tool presentation carts

3. Create poka yokes, etc.
4. Run through new process with operators, get feedback
5. Create new balanced work sheets
6. Meet with swing shift, run through process and get feedback

Sample Flow Kaizen Agenda: Thursday
1. Get the process running
2. Observe and time; rebalance work
3. Review problems with current process
4. Create new kaizen newspaper and attack tasks
5. Observe and time work cycle, make adjustments
6. Create new standard operations; begin work on final report out
7. Review new standard operations with both shifts
8. 5S the area, create chalk or tape outlines on floor to mark new layout
9. Close out kaizen newspaper

Checklist for Moving Assembly Lines
If reconfiguring an assembly line, create a checklist for yourself and carry it with you all day. Your checklist might look like this:
✓ Team members and operators briefed
✓ Sketches of new line and processes distributed

✓ Safety equipment on hand/in use
✓ Maintenance briefed
✓ Materials available to make parts presentation boards, etc.
✓ Ready to photograph the move
✓ Operators trained on new processes
✓ Newly balanced work sheets created
✓ Floor marked off with new layouts
✓ New cycle time/takt time bar chart created
✓ New kaizen newspaper for Thursday, created with the team
✓ New standard operations written for operators
✓ Area update meetings, both shifts
✓ Management meeting preparations

Flow Event Final Presentation Lineup

For the final presentation in a production flow event, organize team members to present the following:

1. Scope and objectives
2. Pre-kaizen measures
3. Takt time calculation
4. Pre-kaizen spaghetti chart
5. Pre-kaizen cycle time/takt time bar chart
6. Post-kaizen layout
7. Post-kaizen cycle time/takt time bar chart
8. Standard operations examples
9. Kaizen implemented examples

10. 5S audit
11. Results summary
12. 30-day homework list

Set-up Reduction Final Presentation Lineup

1. Scope and objectives
2. Setup time bar chart (all observations)
3. Setup time observation sheet
4. Spaghetti chart
5. Improvement ideas
6. External setup checklists – video possibility
7. Internal setup procedure – video possibility
8. Kaizen implemented examples
9. 5S audit
10. Results summary (lead time, setup time, inventory, quality, safety, etc.)
11. 30-day homework list

TPM Event Final Presentation Lineup

1. Scope and objectives
2. Pre-kaizen measures (downtime, throughput, productivity)
3. Equipment diagram and function descriptions
4. OEE calculation
5. Blue Tag summary chart
6. Kaizen newspaper - prioritized
7. Kaizen implemented examples

8. Equipment checklists (daily, weekly, monthly)
9. Autonomous skill matrix
10. 5S audit
11. Results summary
12. 30-day homework list

Business Process

Business Process Pre-Event Checklist

- ✓ Meet with event sponsor, KPO event coordinator
- ✓ Team selected
- ✓ Team packets prepared with relevant data, scope and objectives
- ✓ Process map prepared
- ✓ Pre-event meeting held in target project area
- ✓ Historic data collected (quality, staffing, OT, etc.)
- ✓ Value chain map obtained from KPO or sponsor
- ✓ Pre-event meeting with IT
- ✓ All needed materials available

Kaizen Event Agenda: Business Process

Monday	Training
Tuesday	Discovery
Wednesday	Do
Thursday	Do, Re-do, Document
Friday	Debrief

A Note on Daily BP Agendas

In Business Process events agendas can vary widely, depending on whether the team completes the process map pre-event or schedules this work for Tuesday. The rule of thumb is that if the process map is completed before the kaizen week begins, the project should be selected and tasks assigned by end-of-day Tuesday. If process mapping begins Tuesday morning, the project is finalized by Wednesday noon. Therefore, these agendas should be used as a reminder of all that must be accomplished.

Sample BP Agenda: Tuesday-Wednesday

1. Introduction; review target-area rules
2. Create or review the process map
3. Time observation studies
4. Time observation reports
5. Redeploy teams to pick up missing steps
6. Compute takt time; review list of baseline data to be collected
7. Data collection; brainstorming
8. Collect missing data; document opportunities noticed for waste elimination; review ideas against scope and objectives
9. Create implementation plan
10. Meet with target-area manager

Sample BP Kaizen Agenda: Thursday

1. Split into sub teams
2. Implement plan
3. Document (create new standard work)
4. Create new process map

5. Informal pulse check with target-area associates

BP Final Presentation Lineup
1. Scope and objectives
2. Process map
3. Baseline data
4. Cycle time/takt time bar charts
5. Spaghetti chart
6. Examples of waste, issues, barriers
7. Difficulty/impact matrix
8. Kaizen implemented examples
9. New process map
10. Standard operations example
11. Results summary
12. 30-day homework list

Sigma Kaizen

• Principles & Tools •

Checklists & Agendas
Measure/Analyze, Analyze/Improve/Control

Live Data vs. Dead Data

Dead data is historical process statistics; live data is that which is observed and collected about the process this week or today. In Sigma Kaizen, live data refers to information collected during the Measure/Analyze week or in the interim period between weeks. Dead data is not necessarily worthless information, but it is less valuable than live data.

In general, we use dead data to search for and identify trends. We use live data to guide our work and, ultimately, the decisions we make about specific improvements.

Data Worlds

Defective Data=
Entire part is good or bad
• Product insprection - go/no go
• Delivery- on-time/late
• Invoice- correct/not correct

Defects Data=
Each error or nonconformity is counted
• Number of voids in a weld
• Number of blanks on an order
• Number of errors on a design

Continuous Data=
Measurable Characteristics
• Time to receive payment
• Length of a rotor shaft
• Response Time

- Defective data: The unit either meets or does not meet customer requirements
- Defects data: The number of times a unit fails to meet requirements
- Continuous data: A measurable characteristic that can take on any value

Process Capability

The team will measure process capability (the Z value) in week one, and then return to measure it again at the project's conclusion. Make sure everyone has a good understanding of the data environment (see above) before you proceed with measurements.

Measurement System Analysis

Just as processes have variations, measurements have variation as well. It is critical to identify, therefore, how much variation occurs in the chosen measurement system.

The MSA depends on which data stream you've chosen, as follows:

- Discrete/Attribute (encompassing defective and defect) = Expert re-evaluation, appraiser agreement
- Continuous = Gage R&R

Below is an illustration of all the elements you could potentially evaluate using MSA within the continuous data world.

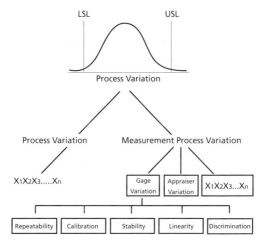

First-Time Yield

When discussing yield, take care to only count *first-time yield*. Rework should not be included in this equation, which is concerned only with the percentage of product that is good the first time through.

Another useful measure is Rolled Throughput Yield, which is a multiplication of the first-time yield of all relevant machines in a process. For instance, if you have a three-machine process, multiply the first-time yield of machine A by first-time yield of machine B, multiplied by the first-time yield of machine C. Or:

FTY (A) x FTY (B) x FTY(C) = RTY

For example: (.99 x .97 x .85 = 0.816) or 82%

Rolled Throughput Yield is an excellent way to assess how well your process line is performing.

Critical to Quality Characteristics

Critical to quality (or CTQ) refers to any characteristic related to form, fit, function or customer expectations. A CTQ is anything required by the customer and any reasonable expectation of that product.

Y = f (X)

Y is the output of the process, which is what we measure in the first week. At the end of week one, and in the interim between weeks, we collect information on the Xs – the inputs to a process that affect the output. These vital few Xs are the items that we need to understand and control. Y = f (X), illustrates the central concept of Six Sigma: outputs are a function of inputs. We must track and understand inputs in order to truly understand and control output.

Quality Map

The quality map details every step in a process, including:

- Specifications
- Materials
- Tools and fixtures used

Principles & Tools

Process Steps	Tool	Pipe Before	Pipe After
Specs/Quality Standards	Flare on tube end indicates full insertion of tool meeting design criteria for return bend insertion		
Gauging Control Method	Design specification on drawings		
Tooling & Fixturing	Flare tool		
Defects Found / Known Problems	Unequal length and flare alignment		
Defect Causes	Operator variability		
Gap Analysis	No measurable quantity for flare size. No minimum or maximum tube length below flare dimension. Possible red tool to define length.		

Gaps include any element without adequate control or anything that is blatantly missing. A gap might be a step in the process that has a specification but no control method; or a gap might be the fact that operators don't check that output is within specification. A gap might also refer to an inadequate gauge.

Business Process Flow Map

This map reveals the movement of documents and information through an organization, including hand-offs, loops and rework. Essential elements of the business process flow map include:

- Clearly identified responsibilities of each process owner
- All handoffs between business sections identified
- Identification of who does what over time

When creating a business process map, make sure there is agreement on the meaning of each symbol and shape. A diamond often indicates a decision juncture and a rectangle indicates physical action. Between action items, a straight line indicates physical movement and a dotted line or lightening bolt shows an electronic transfer.

Fishbone Diagram

This is a brainstorming tool to identify all potential root causes. Have the team use Post-It Notes or some other vehicle to silently write down each potential reason for the defect, using one idea per note. Then find the common ideas and put them along the same rib: materials, measurement, methods, manpower, environment, machines.

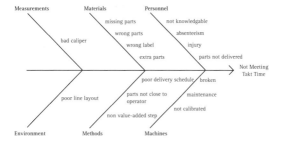

Post the fishbone diagram for all to see; it becomes very useful in the comparative analysis.

Comparative Analysis

This explores what the defect is and what it is not; helping the team filter down to the vital few root causes through comparison. If told that a defect occurs "all the time," ask, "Does it occur every month? Every week? Every day? Every hour?" Only specific, verifiable data will lead us to the root.

Defect Statement: What is the defect?		What is the unit?		
Specifying Statement	Is	Is Not	Differences	Changes
What	What specific object(s) has the defect? What is the specific defect?	What similar object(s) could have the defect, but does not? What other defects could be observed, but are not?		
Where	Where is the defective object observed (geographically)? Where is the defect on the object?	Where else could the defective object be observed, but in not? Where else could the defect be on the object, but in not?		
When	When was the defective object firsdt obsrved (clock/calendar)? When observed since then? When in object's life cycle/history was the defect first observed?	When else could the defective object have been first observed, but was not? What other times could have the defective object been observed, but was not? When else could defective object have been observed in it's life cycle, but was not?		
How Big How May	How many objects have the defect? How many defects are on each object? What is the size of the defect? What has been the trend?	How many objects could have had the defect, but do not? How many defects could there be on each object, but are not? What size could the defect be, but is not? What other trends could have been expected, but were not observed?		

Evaluate Differences (possible causes)
Test possible causes against the IS and IS NOT to determine most probable causes:
If "X" is the root cause, how does it explain both the IS and IS NOT information?
What assumptions have to be true to explain the IS and IS NOT?

What is different or unique in, on, around or about an IS compared to its IS NOT? (list each difference separately against each IS and IS NOT statement)

What has changed in, on, around or about the difference or defect? (list and date each difference separately against each IS and IS NOT statement)

Use a blank form, but use these questions to help guide the discussion.

Pareto

Pareto illustrates the rate of frequency for each defect category. It is a focusing tool, helping to define the Sigma Kaizen project. It should be demonstrated to the team, though its real use may occur before the event begins.

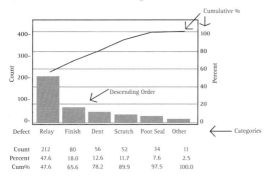

Defect	Relay	Finish	Dent	Scratch	Poor Seal	Other
Count	212	80	56	52	34	11
Percent	47.6	18.0	12.6	11.7	7.6	2.5
Cum%	47.6	65.6	78.2	89.9	97.5	100.0

Project Selection Bounding Sheet

To focus in on the precise scope and objectives of your project, use the project-bounding sheet illustrated below, which contains questions that need to be answered. Use a blank project-bounding sheet to work through possible Sigma Kaizen projects until you find one that measures up to all criteria. Review the completed project-bounding sheet with the team to illustrate why the project is important.

Business Problem:
(Describe the problem from a business perspective and why we care)
- Variation in width affecting downstream weight and centering
- Longevity of part can be affected by width and centering causing warranty problems

Business Metrics affected:
(What business metrics will change if the problem is eliminated)

Unit Statement:
(What is the unit/product/product line)
- Part # 175

Defect Statement:
(specifically, what is the defect and how is it measured)
- Width, cut (Opti System)

Data availability:
(what sources of data are available / How readily)
- Individual measurements in database which can be used in Excel
- Available on demand

Savings Potential:
(what is the total size of the pie and how much will this project address)
- $92,000

Team Members:

Sponsor:

As you work through project selection, make certain the work aligns with overall business objectives. Fill out the charter form, including business objectives and deliverables, in plain language.

Charter Form

Description:	Shot Saw Slabbing Process
Business Objective:	Improve Slab Quality
Deliverable:	50% Improvement from Baseline
Project Y/Defect:	Rough Surface on Slab Face

Financial:	Estimated	Actual	
	$800,000 - $1,000,000		

Timing:	Started	Completed	Implemented
Sponsors:	10/26/00	12/8/00	

Project Leader:	Pat Mitchell
Mentor:	David Beal
Process Owner:	Jay Esmay

When deciding the project deliverables, be careful to identify real savings. Real savings for Sigma Kaizen are usually expressed in material and output. Saving material by eliminating scrap and improving yield can be counted in dollars. And increasing output in your target area, which creates new revenue, always counts in dollars.

Sigma Kaizen

Principles & Tools

• **Checklists & Agendas** •
Measure/Analyze, Analyze/Improve/Control

Measure/Analyze

Pre-event Meeting With KPO
The pre-event meeting with the KPO event coordinator and the project sponsor should cover each of the following:

1. Team packets
2. Discuss objectives
3. Background on the area
4. Obtain historical data
5. Target area meeting?
6. Support staff assigned?

Team Packets
Each member of the team should receive a packet of information that includes:

- Completed Sigma Kaizen charter form
- Area layout
- Value stream map
- List of area rules and safety procedures
- Baseline data, including:
  - Yield
  - Scrap
  - Rework
  - Warranty/customer return
  - Process capability: specifications, tolerance
  - Blueprints of the component in question
  - Standard operations (if existing)

Pre-Sigma Kaizen Event Checklist
- ✓ Team selected
- ✓ Packet prepared
- ✓ Pre-event meeting in area
- ✓ Historical data collected
- ✓ Area visited
- ✓ Support personnel contacted
- ✓ Measurement system identified
- ✓ Computer available with Minitab

Measure/Analyze Event Agenda

Monday	Training & Scope
Tuesday	Mapping
Wednesday	Collecting
Thursday	Root Cause Analysis
Friday	Debrief

Monday Training Agenda
Be prepared to teach the following modules:
1. LeanSigma methodology
2. Sigma Kaizen event overview
3. Bounding Sheet
4. Charter
5. Mapping: overview of enhanced spaghetti, quality or business process flow
6. Collection: Measurement System Analysis, process capability
7. Root cause analysis: fishbone, comparative analysis

Checklist for Tuesday

Make sure all is ready before leaving on Monday evening.

- ✓ CAD drawing of area obtained for spaghetti map
- ✓ Forms prepared for quality mapping
- ✓ Butcher paper on hand (or another method for enlarging the quality map)
- ✓ Copies of standard operation sheets available for everyone, prior to mapping
- ✓ Comparative analysis sheets ready
- ✓ Poster-sized comparative analysis (3'x4' or larger) obtained
- ✓ Historical data evaluated and prepared for presentation
- ✓ Macro flow chart of process, split into chunks for sub teams ready

Checklist for Wednesday

Before leaving Tuesday evening, go over this checklist to be sure you're ready for Wednesday.

- ✓ Measurement System Analysis type(s) identified
- ✓ Outsiders to participate in each MSA (operators, etc.) identified
- ✓ Area manager meeting held; clearance obtained for operators to participate in MSA
- ✓ Computer with Minitab loaded and ready
- ✓ MSA forms – paper or digital – prepared
- ✓ Office supplies acquired, including tags, markers, etc.

- ✓ Ready to collect live data (forms are prepared, etc.)
- ✓ Experts lined up, if needed, for team interviews

Checklist for Thursday
- ✓ Necessary parts scheduled for production during MSA
- ✓ Experts ready to come in for team interviews
- ✓ Resources (maintenance, IT) lined up to help the team complete a timeline for comparative analysis

Measure/Analyze Final Presentation Lineup
Organize the team to present this highly structured presentation, which should follow this format:

1. Sigma Kaizen Charter
2. Team members
3. Picture of part or process
4. Enhanced Spaghetti Map
5. Quality Map (if applicable)
6. Business Process Flow Map (if applicable)
7. Pareto of Opportunities
8. Process Capability
9. Cause and Effect Diagram
10. Comparative Analysis
11. Key Quality Control Tools
12. 30-Day Homework List

Analyze/Improve/Control

In the interim between Sigma Kaizen project weeks, the team leader will be busy collecting additional data and doing preliminary analysis. The results of this should be reported to the team in a memo before the final week begins.

To remain on track, meet with the KPO Event Coordinator and event sponsor again before the Analyze/Improve/Control week to discuss opportunities. A new packet should be prepared for team members, as well.

Pre-event Meeting
1. Team packets prepared
2. New data in packets
3. Target-area meeting held
4. Support staff assigned
5. Logistics ready (food, etc.)
6. Team room available

Analyze/Improve/Control Agenda

Monday	Review & Training
Tuesday	Analyze & Improve
Wednesday	Improve
Thursday	Verify
Friday	Debrief

Monday's Training Agenda
1. Quality tools (including box plots, run charts, Pareto, histogram, etc.)
2. Hypothesis testing*
3. Regression*
4. Risk assessment
5. Improvement methods (mistake proofing, elimination of root cause, optimization)
6. DOE/Experimentation*
7. Control plans
8. Review of entire process: MAIC

These training modules are taught on a high level. Discuss the overall concepts; do not explain how to perform these tasks.

Checklist for Tuesday
This day is dedicated to finding the root cause of the variation through careful analysis of live data. Be prepared to create Histograms and Box Plots and lead the team through regression and hypothesis testing. Before leaving Monday, make sure you're ready.
✓ All necessary data entered in Minitab
✓ Risk assessment and root cause/improvement forms prepared

Checklist for Wednesday

This is the most active day in the week. Be prepared before leaving the building Tuesday.

✓ Maintenance and/or IT resources ready
✓ All necessary tools lined up
✓ All necessary materials ready

Checklist for Thursday

The main objectives for Thursday are running the process, correcting the process, running it again – through several iterations – and documenting the changes.

✓ Ready to write standard operations
✓ Meeting scheduled with process owner

Analyze/Improve/Control

Final Presentation Lineup

1. Kaizen Charter
2. Process Capability
3. Summary of Measure/Analyze presentation
4. Analyze Summary
5. Risk Assessment
6. Before & After: Process Capability
7. Improve Summary
8. Proof of Improvement
9. Control Plan
10. Kaizen 30-Day Goals

Sigma Kaizen: Control

The team leader's most pressing task is to make sure that the 30-day homework list is completed. This is one of the best control methods available.

The team leader should also conduct **30-60-90-day audits** with the process owner and a KPO representative to review area performance and completion status of homework items. If applicable, you could use Statistical Process Control (SPC) to monitor the process during this period.

Team visits

Create a schedule in which a team member visits the target area every day for the first 10 days following the event. The visits should be no more than 30 minutes or so and each visit should have a specific purpose, such as completing an item off the homework list, checking process against standard operations, conducting spot quality checks and answering questions. Site visits can then be scaled back to three times a week, then twice a week until the area is stable and the homework list is completed.

Value Stream Map

Within two weeks of the event, the team leader and event coordinator should test the target area to see that the original kaizen gains are being realized. If not, corrective action should be taken. If the gains are being realized, update the company's value stream map as soon as possible in order to lock in everyone's expectations of the process.

Finally, call a **30-day follow up meeting** with the original team, the management sponsor, your KPO representative and any other interested parties. Have a graph prepared to show the area's improvement and be prepared to formally close out the 30-day homework list.

Design for LeanSigma®

• Principles & Tools •

Checklists & Agendas
Voice of the Customer, Design Kaizen,
Production Preparation

Customer Focus

In Design for LeanSigma, *customer focus* means the customer's requirements and desires guide the work – not engineering or marketing or manufacturing. The voice-of-the-customer data collected in a project's initial phases will inform design, cost and functionality.

Managed Creativity

The challenge of Design for LeanSigma is that it requires wild creativity on a strict deadline. Team leaders make this happen with Managed Creativity, which is a set of tools, such as Seven Alternatives and Word Pairs. Use these tools to drive the team to generate a lot of ideas, get everyone participating and use the collective intelligence of the team to create more and better ideas.

Try-storming

This terms simply means creating three-dimensional mock-ups of ideas, using leftover wood, duct tape, PVC pipe and other scraps. Try-storming shows us where the flaws in our perceptions might be and encourages a deeper understanding of any product or process.

When brainstorming has run its course, the next step should always be try-storming because Design for LeanSigma pushes teams to "pull the trigger" fast, and we need these quick mockups to understand all aspects of a project.

Creativity Before Capital

Any company that accepts using capital for new products and processes generally ends up with expensive machines purchased from catalogues. The machinery might be incredibly fast and powerful, but it will probably not be designed to work to the process takt time or fit the working conditions. This often leads to inventory build-up between processes as those fast machines produce more parts than are needed in order to appease the accounting department, which approved purchase of the machine based on usage targets. Following the principle of creativity before capital, teams are encouraged to rethink processes from scratch, to imagine new ways of accomplishing old tasks without spending any money.

Design for Profitability

Producing profitability at the short-term instead of chasing an optimistic, long-term forecast is at the heart of this principle. If volume projections show the first year's demand at 100, increasing to 500 by year three, the conventional wisdom would be to build capacity and production processes for 500 per year. Design for Profitability tells us to design a 100-volume-per-year process to meet cost, quality and capacity targets with minimum capital and cost. We achieve 500 units per year – assuming the forecasts are eventually realized – by duplicating the process and improving it at each repetition. If the volume projections fail to materialize, we are not locked into a huge dead investment at 500 per year.

House of Quality

This tool helps teams visualize and focus on the needs of the customer. The HOQ brings all the decision-making inputs onto a single form and defines the critical interactions of those inputs. It will help the team identify the relative difficulty and importance of design characteristics. There are many methods for building a House of Quality, from specialized software programs to simple flip charts and tape. Until an organization has internal expertise on the HOQ tools, it is strongly recommended that an outside expert lead the team.

This is a general outline of the HOQ, showing how it translates customer needs into product specifications:

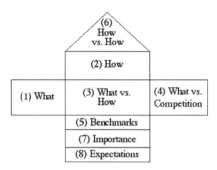

Always begin HOQ work with an overview of the data being entered and its relationship to the whole. This is important even if everyone says they know the tool, in order to establish a common understanding of the terms and usage.

Word Pairs
Use simple noun-verb pairings to describe functionality in order to obtain simple, to-the-point descriptions. For example, a chair:
1. Supports weight
2. Provides comfort
3. Looks good

Whittling ideas on functionality down to the few, critical words help a team focus on essential product behaviors and minimize core variation.

Examples From Nature
This is usually a brief exercise designed to open

minds and draw team members along unique paths. When considering how to support a heavy weight, for example, ask the team to brainstorm how nature does this. The list you write might include spider webs, cocoons, tree roots. Keep examples posted to encourage the team to return to these ideas.

Seven Alternatives

This is an idea-broadening exercise in which team members sketch seven alternatives for a process or component. There will be team members who swear there is only one way to screw in a light bulb, and it's the team leader's job to answer that assertion with four or five variations on a single task. All ideas should be sketched, not written, on the Alternatives at a Glance sheet.

Support the Vision of the Preferred Manufacturing										
Project Name _____ Assembly Operation Name/# _____ Date _____										
Method 10	Method 9	Method 8	Method 7	Method 6	Method 5	Method 4	Method 3	Method 2	Method 1	Sequence
										Material Process Sketch
										Sketch of Work Method
				NA						Sketch of Measuring Gauge (Poka Yoke)
				NA	NA			NA	NA	Sketch of Required Tools
			NA			NA	NA		NA	Sketch of Jigs or Fixtures (Hanedashi)

Principles & Tools

T-Chart

This simple chart guides the team to list the advantages and disadvantages of each design alternative, along with cost calculations. This is the bridge between Seven Alternatives and the Concept Evaluation form. Don't complete a T-Chart on all seven alternatives. Instead, guide the team through a brief discussion of the alternatives and pick those that will continue on to the T-Chart and then the Concept Evaluation.

Proposal Name:
Proposal Number

Advantage	Changes	Disadvantages	Change	How to Overcome
Reduce Cost	9.00	Investment for mold for cover	$5000	
Reduce Number of parts	9 to 1	Different material has unknown durability	Steel to Plastic	Perform durability test
Reduce material & weight				
Saves assembly time	33 sec's			
Net Tooling Cost Change: 5,000		Other Cost Changes: (Describe) Labor Savings $.40		
Net Piece Cost Change: $9.00		Volumes:	Implementation Date:	

Concept Evaluation Worksheet

This worksheet helps evaluate concepts in the design phase. List the most important customer requirements and assign each a value from 1-5, depending on importance to the overall product. Ideas are then evaluated against the weighted customer requirements and potential costs. The resulting value ratio shows the ability to satisfy customer requirements divided by the potential cost of the idea. Cocept Evaluation Worksheet:

Relative Importance Force Rank Scale 1-5	Select: Evaluation Criteria HOQ technical characteristics	Best Proposals Rate From (0) to (10) compared to (5) Present Design							
		Proposal current design	Proposal 1	Proposal 4	Proposal 5	Proposal	Proposal	Proposal	Proposal
5	Light weight	5/25	8/40	6/30	7/35				
4	Durable/Strength	5/20	5/20	5/20	1/4				
4	Vibration Resistance	5/20	3/12	1/4	6/24				
2	Easy to Maintain	5/10	7/14	5/10	3/6				
Weighted Function Totals		75	86	64	69				
Piece Cost Change		-	-9.00	-1.00	-3.00				
Total Piece Cost		100.00	91.00	99.00	97.00				
Value Ratio = Function/Cost		.75	.95	.65	.71				
Tooling Costs			50,000						
Engeenering Costs									
Model Year Implementation			2001						

Design Assessment

In a Design Kaizen, also known as design for manufacturability, this form guides the assessment of designs in consideration. Using the Design Assessment, the team will define the number of parts, work through the potential to reduce parts and define the theoretical minimum number of parts.

The assessment asks three critical questions noted under "Minimum Parts Test":

1. Does the part need to move (relative to other parts already installed)?
2. Does it need to be made of a different material than its adjoining parts?
3. Does it ever need to be separated from the adjacent part?

If the answer is yes to any of these questions, two parts are necessary. If the answer is no to all three, it can be a single part.

Item	Qty	Minimum Parts Test			Theoretical Part Count	Assembly Time	
		Move	Material	Separate		Current Design	New Design
Stand-off screws	4	N	N	N	0		
End plate	1	N	N	N	0		
LVDT stand-offs	4	N	N	N	0		
Base	1	N	N	Y	1	33	3
LBDT	1	N	Y	Y	1		3
Cover	1	N	N	Y	1	22	3
Cover Screws	4	N	N	N	0		
Total parts	16				3		
Total time (sec's)						55	9

Fishbone Diagram
In a Production Preparation week, the Fishbone Diagram is used to sketch out all the pieces of a product and the order in which they are put together.

Process Worksheet
This is a pictorial representation of each of the physical transformation steps defined in the fishbone diagram, along with a written description of

each, as the current process exists.

Name:	*Cinch cutter*		Date:	*February 3, 2000*
Part Description:	*Shank*		Process Criteria:	1 - Takt Time
Part Number:	Y2K-020300			2 - One-Piece Flow
				3 - Pull System

080	070	060	050	040	030	020	010	Sequence
								Process Sketch
SPOT	MILL FLAT	CUT OFF	TURN O.D.'s	TAP	DRILL	SPOT	FACE	Operation Description

Alternatives at a Glance

Sketch out all the alternatives on a single sheet like this whenever possible. Seeing the variety of combinations available on one page encourages new thinking.

New Process Alternatives Evaluation

Each of the seven process alternatives should be judged against lean criteria using the process evaluation, pictured next page. The team chooses the most promising alternatives and scores each against the most relevant lean criteria. Some of the lean criteria should be used in every evaluation, such as "meets takt time," "one-piece flow" and "minimal capital." Use your judgment in selecting additional criteria for each process step.

Evaluation Criteria	1	2	3	4	5	6	7	8	9	10	Sum
Meet takt time	3	3	5	5							
One-piece flow	4	5	5	5							
Minimum ooperator involvement	5	5	5	5							
Hane dashi	1	1	4	3							
Poka yoke	1	1	3	2							
Minimal capital	1	1	5	5							
100% gauging	3	3	2	3							
Value-adding operation	5	5	5	5							
Change over	4	4	3	3							
No tool room maintenance	4	3	3	3							
Tooling cost	3	3	2	2							
Erogonomics & safity	3	3	3	2							
Simple as possible	2	1	4	3							
Standard equipment	4	3	3	3							
Process capability	3	2	4	4							
Know/existing process	5	5	5	5							
Future challenge	3	3	3	3							
Maintenance free machines	3	3	3	3							
Technology advantage	4	3	5	4							
Jidoka	3	3	3	3							
Minimum time to develop	4	4	4	4							
	69	65	84	80							
	3	4	1	2							

If the team is working on a smaller project with a limited number of steps, this evaluation can be accomplished as an entire team. For more complex projects, such as a vehicle, the team should be broken into groups and each given a chunk of the whole.

Process at a Glance

This is a sketched illustration of each of the final transformation steps, in correct production sequence, showing work methods, measuring gauges, cutting tools and jigs or fixtures.

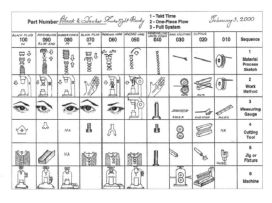

Design for LeanSigma®

Principles & Tools

• **Checklists & Agendas** •

Voice of the Customer, Design Kaizen,
Production Preparation

Voice of the Customer

Pre-event Checklist

✓ Team selected, notified
✓ Agenda sent to team members, with objectives
✓ Initial customer data collected, analyzed
✓ Competitive products collected
✓ Internal data on competitive or existing products

Kaizen Week Agenda

Monday	Training
Tuesday	House of Quality
Wednesday	Concept Development
Thursday	Refine and Select
Friday	Debrief

Monday Training Agenda

1. House of Quality
2. Translating customer requirements to specifications
3. Comparison to competitive products
4. Identifying technical requirements
5. Setting target specifications
6. Developing concepts using managed creativity

Checklist for Tuesday

Before leaving the building Monday evening, be prepared for Tuesday's work.

✓ Blank House of Quality ready to hang
✓ Tuesday agenda complete

Tuesday Agenda

- Develop customer requirements from surveys and data
- Weight criteria by importance
- Translate customer requirements into design characteristics
- Evaluate design characteristics vs. customer requirements
- Establish design characteristic weighting
- Competitive analysis
- Set target specifications

Checklist for Wednesday

✓ Reams of paper
✓ Colored pens
✓ Plenty of wall space to hang pictures
✓ Materials and tools to make concept models (clay, cardboard, duct tape, etc.)
✓ Wednesday agenda completed

Wednesday Agenda

- Develop concepts
- Group concepts into families

- Narrow concepts to one or two choices
- Create models

Checklist for Thursday
- ✓ Modeling supplies replenished
- ✓ Outside reviewers prepared to come in
- ✓ Objectives reviewed, remaining tasks listed

Thursday Agenda
- Continued modeling and mock-ups
- Best design selection
- Outside design review
- Cost analysis
- Go-forward plan

Final Presentation Lineup: VOC
1. Objectives
2. Customer verbatims
3. House of Quality
4. Concept development
5. Seven alternatives
6. Concept evaluation sheet
7. Models
8. Review feedback
9. Implementation plan
10. Results summary (if redesign)

Design Kaizen

Pre-event Checklist
, Team selected, notified
, Agenda sent to team members, with objectives
, Sponsor identified
, Meeting with KPO event coordinator
, Competitive products collected
, Mock-up or current models collected

Kaizen Week Agenda: Design Kaizen
Monday	Train
Tuesday	Tear Down
Wednesday	Create Concepts
Thursday	Mock and Review
Friday	Debrief

Monday Training Agenda
1. Design for Manufacturability
2. Design assessment
3. Parts reduction
4. Guidelines for ease of assembly
5. Parts presentation
6. Parts handling
7. Parts insertion
8. Parts fastening
9. Product variation
10. Mistake proofing
11. Raw material choices

Checklist for Tuesday

Before leaving Monday, be prepared for Tuesday's activities:

✓ Technical characteristics ready to present
✓ Products in team room
✓ Competitors' products in team room
✓ Tools and work space ready (e.g. table covered in paper)
✓ Agenda created

Tuesday's Agenda

- Tear down existing products and lay out
- Fishbone
- Determine number of parts
- Analyze current product for parts reduction potential
- Tear down and analyze competition
- Evaluate competition against customer criteria

Checklist for Wednesday

✓ Collect all materials for mock up, such as wood, duct tape, clay, paper, etc.
✓ Create agenda

Wednesday Agenda

- Define concept design
- Document advantages of new design
- Cost estimates
- Evaluate alternatives

- Construct mock ups

Checklist for Thursday
- ✓ Replenish materials for mock-up
- ✓ Outside evaluators invited
- ✓ Agenda created

The agenda for Thursday should include:
- Finalize mock ups
- Evaluate/review with external groups
- Select final design and incorporate feedback
- Develop cost analysis
- Develop production plan

Final Presentation Lineup for Design Kaizen
1. Fishbone diagram
2. Design assessment
3. Competitive analysis
4. Examples from nature
5. Representative T-Charts
6. Concept Evaluation worksheet
7. Demonstrate product mock ups
8. Cost analysis
9. Production plan (if appropriate)
10. Implementation plan

Production Preparation

Pre-event Checklist
✓ Collect information on volume/seasonal fluctuations
✓ Select team
✓ Distribute memo
✓ Meet with KPO, check out work room, tools, materials
✓ Identify and meet with sponsor

Production Preparation Kaizen Agenda
Monday	Train
Tuesday	Evaluate
Wednesday	Innovate
Thursday	Simulate
Friday	Debrief

Monday Training Agenda
1. Design for Profitability
2. Building Quality into the Process
3. Equipment Planning
4. Trial Evaluation
5. Steps of Production Preparation

Checklist for Tuesday

Before leaving Monday, make sure the following is ready for Tuesday:

- ✓ Alternatives-at-a-glance forms available
- ✓ Agenda created

Tuesday's Agenda

- • Complete fishbone diagram
- • Choose targeted process steps
- • Develop seven alternatives for every targeted process step

Checklist for Wednesday

- ✓ All modeling materials are on hand
- ✓ Agenda created for Wednesday, with sponsor and event coordinator

Wednesday Agenda

- • Evaluate alternatives
- • Choose the best alternative
- • Model each operation
- • Design workstations
- • Develop materials presentation

Checklist for Thursday

- ✓ Building materials replenished
- ✓ Prototypes on hand to run simulated operations
- ✓ Agenda created

Thursday Agenda
- Simulate and refine workstations
- Link all workstations, simulate assembly
- Balance workload against takt time
- Create standard operations
- Set staffing levels
- Document tools, fixtures, workstation design

Final Presentation Lineup Production Prep
1. Objectives
2. Fishbone
3. Alternatives (examples)
4. Evaluation of alternatives
5. Takt time calculation
6. Layout of line
7. Staffing
8. Standard operations example
9. Sample of material presentation/work station design
10. Equipment procurement plan
11. Implementation plan
12. Results summary

Glossary

A

Abnormality Management
The ability to see and respond to an abnormality (any violation of standard operations) in a timely manner.

Andon
A visual signal. Typically, a light mounted on a machine or line to indicate a potential problem or work stoppage.

Autonomation
English translation of Jidoka. Imparting human intelligence to a machine so that it automatically stops when a problem arises.

B

Balanced Plant
A plant where all available capacity is balanced exactly to market demand.

Bottleneck
An area or workstation in a manufacturing environment that limits throughput of the entire process.

C

Chaku-chaku Line
Meaning load-load in Japanese, this describes a work cell where machines off-load parts automatically so that operators can take a piece directly from one machine to the next without waiting.

Change Agent
A person whose demonstrated mission is to move from the now state, or batch and queue, to the future ideal state: lean manufacturing. One who leads cultural change in an organization.

Cellular Manufacturing
An alignment of machines in correct process sequence, where operators remain within the cell and materials are presented to them from outside.

Constraint
A workstation or a process that limits the output of the entire system.

Continuous Improvement
The commitment to creating a better product, work environment and business, every day.

Cycle Time
The time it takes an operator to complete one full repetition of work. Globally, it is the time it takes before the cycle repeats itself. See Operator Cycle Time, Machine Cycle Time.

D

3Ds
Dirty, dangerous, difficult.

E

Elemental Time
Time allotted to a specific operational step, within standard work.

External Set-up
Elements of tooling set-up that can be performed safely while the machine is still running.

F

Five S (5S)
The primary conditioning discipline for kaizen, the five Ss are defined as: Seiri, to segregate and discard. Seiton, to arrange and identify. Seiso, to clean and inspect daily. Seiketsu, to revisit frequently, and Shitsuke, to motivate to sustain. In English, 5S is commonly translated as sort, set in order, sweep, standardize and sustain.

G

Global Production System
An expansion of the Toyota Production System, this is a strategy to enable lean manufacturing using kaizen methodology.

H

Hanedashi
A device that allows a machine to automatically unload a part without waiting for an operator.

Heijunka
Production smoothing; creating a build sequence that is determined by SKU average demand.

I

Internal Set-up
Elements of tooling set-up that must be performed while the machine is not in motion.

Inventory
Usually the highest cost category, inventory is all raw materials, purchased parts, work-in-progress and finished goods that are not yet sold to a customer.

J

Jidoka
See "autonomation." Japanese term for transferring human intelligence to a machine.

Just In Time (JIT)
Manufacturing what is needed, when it is needed, in the quantity it is needed.

K

Kaikaku
Radical improvement, usually in a business process, that affects the future value stream.

Kaizen
A combination of two Japanese words Kai (change) and Zen (good). Usually defined as "continuous improvement."

Kaizen Breakthrough
A time-sensitive, rapid-deployment methodology that employs a focused, team-based approach. Continuous improvement.

Kanban
Visual signal. Typically a re-order card or other method of triggering the pull system, based on actual usage of material. It should be located for use at the point of manufacturing.

L

Lead Time
The amount of time required to produce a single product, from the time of customer order to shipping.

Lean Manufacturing
Using the minimum amount of total resources — man, materials, money, machines, etc. — to produce a product and deliver it on time.

M

Machine Automatic Time
The time it takes for a machine to produce one unit, exclusive of loading and unloading.

Machine Cycle Time
The time it takes for a machine to produce one unit, including the time it takes to load and unload.

Muda
Any activity that adds to cost without adding to the value of the product.

Mura
Variations in process quality, cost and delivery

Muri
Unreasonableness; demand exceeds capacity.

N

Nagara System
Accomplishing two or more activities with one motion.

Non-Value Added
Any activity that adds cost without adding value
to the product or process.

O

One-touch Exchange of Dies
The reduction of die set-up activities down to a
single step.

One-piece Flow
A manufacturing philosophy which supports the
movement of product from one workstation to
the next, one piece at a time, without allowing
inventory to build up in between.

Operator Cycle Time
The time it takes for a person to complete a
predetermined sequence of operations, inclusive

of loading and unloading, exclusive of time spent
waiting.

P

Pacemaker
A technique for pacing a process to takt time.

Policy Deployment
Matching the strategic business goals of an organization to its available resources. Communicating

those goals throughout the organization and linking everyone to the same objectives.

Poka Yoke
A Japanese word for mistake proofing, a poka yoke device prevents a human error from affecting a machine or process; prevents operator mistakes from becoming defects.

Point Kaizen
An improvement activity intensely directed at a single workstation, performed quickly by two or three specialists. Typically follows a full-blown kaizen event.

Process Capacity Table
A chart primarily used in a machining environment that compares machine load to available capacity.

Production Smoothing
A method of production scheduling that, over a period of time, takes the fluctuation of customer demand out of manufacturing. Producing every part, every day.

Q

Quality Function Deployment
A methodology in which a cross-functional team reaches consensus about final product specifica-

tions, in accord with the wishes of the customer.

Sensei
A revered master or teacher.

Set-up Reduction
Reducing the amount of downtime during changeover from the last good piece to the first good piece of the next order.

Single-minute Exchange of Dies (SMED)
From the last good part to the first good part on the new set-up accomplished in anything less than 10 minutes. AKA "Single-digit set-up."

Standard Operation
The best combination of people and machines utilizing the minimum amount of labor, space, inventory and equipment.

Standard Work
Pre-determined sequence of tasks for the operator to complete within takt time.

Standard Work Combination Sheet
A document showing the sequence of production steps assigned to a single operator. It is used to

illustrate the best combination of worker and machine.

Standard Work Layout
A diagram of a work station or cell showing how standard work is accomplished.

Standard Work in Progress
Minimum material required to complete one cycle of operator work without delay.

Stop-the-line Authority
When abnormalities occur, workers have power to stop the process and prevent the defect or variation from being passed along.

Sub-Optimization
Optimizing each piece of equipment; keeping all machines running, no matter the cost or consequence. Typically this inflates the number-one cost of production: material.

Supermarket
A shop floor, line-side location where parts are sorted and made ready for presentation to operators.

T

Takt Time
The total net daily operating time divided by the

total daily customer demand.

Throughput
The rate at which the entire system generates money.

Time-Based Strategy
Organizing business objectives around economy-of-time principles.

Toyota Production System
Based on some of the first principles of Henry Ford, this describes the philosophies of one of the world's most successful companies. The foundation of TPS is production smoothing, the supports are just-in-time and jidoka.

V

Value Added
Any activity that transforms a product or service to meet the customer need.

Value Analysis
Evaluating the total lead-time and value-added time to identify the percentage spent in value added activities.

Value Stream Map (or Value Chain Map)
A visual picture of how material and information flows from suppliers, through manufacturing, to the customer. It includes calculations of total

cycle time and value-added time. Typically written for the current state of the value chain and the future, to indicate where the business is going.

Visual Controls
Creating standards in the workplace that make it obvious if anything is out of order.

Visual Management
System enabling anyone to quickly spot abnormalities in the workplace, regardless of their knowledge of the process.

W

Work-in-Process (WIP)
Inventory waiting between operation steps.

Work Sequence
The correct steps the operator takes, in the order in which they should be taken.

Notes